The Department of Homeland Security

Fletcher Haulley
AR B.L.: 10.1 Alt.: 1488
Points: 2.0   MG

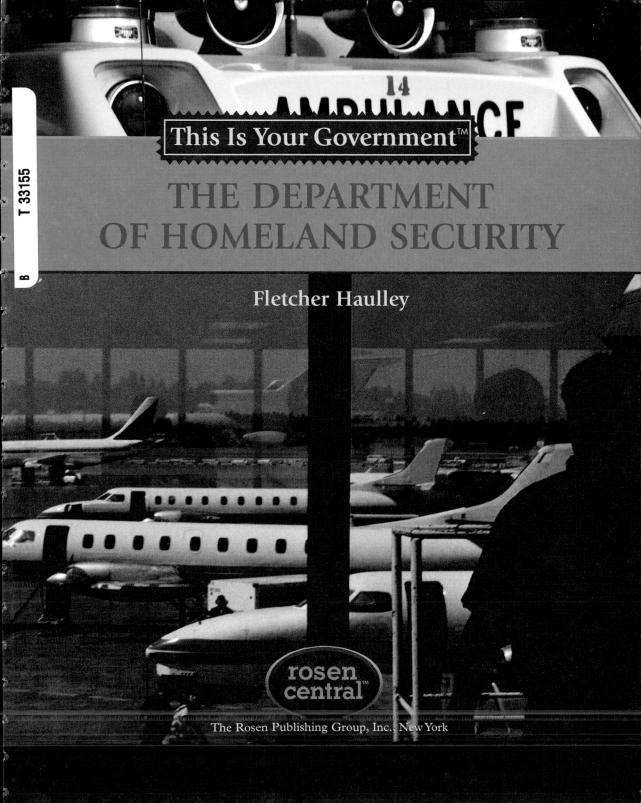

This Is Your Government™

THE DEPARTMENT OF HOMELAND SECURITY

Fletcher Haulley

rosen central™

The Rosen Publishing Group, Inc., New York

To my family

Published in 2006 by The Rosen Publishing Group, Inc.
29 East 21st Street, New York, NY 10010

Copyright © 2006 by The Rosen Publishing Group, Inc.

First Edition

Library of Congress Cataloging-in-Publication Data

Haulley, Fletcher.
The Department of Homeland Security / Fletcher Haulley.—1st ed.
    v. cm.—(This is your government)
Includes bibliographical references and index.
Contents: The history of homeland security—Important figures in homeland security—How the Department of Homeland Security works—The future of homeland security.
ISBN 1-4042-0209-9 (lib. bdg.)
ISBN 1-4042-0662-0 (pbk. bdg.)
1. United States. Dept. of Homeland Security—Juvenile literature. 2. Terrorism—United States—Prevention—Juvenile literature. 3. National security—United States—Juvenile literature. [1. United States. Dept. of Homeland Security. 2. Terrorism. 3. National security. 4. Civil defense.]
I. Title. II. Series.
HV6432.4.H38 2005
353.3'0973—dc22

003027580

Manufactured in the United States of America

On the cover: Left to right: Secretary of Defense Donald Rumsfeld; Vice President Dick Cheney; President George W. Bush; former Secretary of Homeland Security Tom Ridge; and Secretary of Homeland Security Michael Chertoff.

CONTENTS

Introduction

When Islamic terrorists hijacked four commercial planes and crashed three of them into the World Trade Center in New York City and the Pentagon near Washington, D.C., on September 11, 2001, it became clear that United States soil was not the safe, protected place it was long thought to be. The tragic events of that day were not the first signs of America's vulnerability to terrorism. However, these were the first attacks to make Americans feel as if their lives could be changed instantly and forever by members of terrorist groups. The list of casualties was long on that crystal clear day in September, and it called into question the entire American defense system. It also left Americans wondering where the next attack would come from and what peaceful place might next be turned into a scene of carnage.

Department of Homeland Security Organization Chart

CABINET MEMBERS

Secretary of Agriculture	Secretary of Commerce	Secretary of Defense	Secretary of Education	Secretary of Energy	Secretary of Health and Human Services	Secretary of Homeland Security	Secretary of Housing and Urban Development

Deputy Secretary

Undersecretary Management	Undersecretary Science and Technology	Undersecretary Information Analysis and Infrastructure Protection
U.S. Coast Guard	U.S. Secret Service	Bureau of Citizenship and Immigration Services

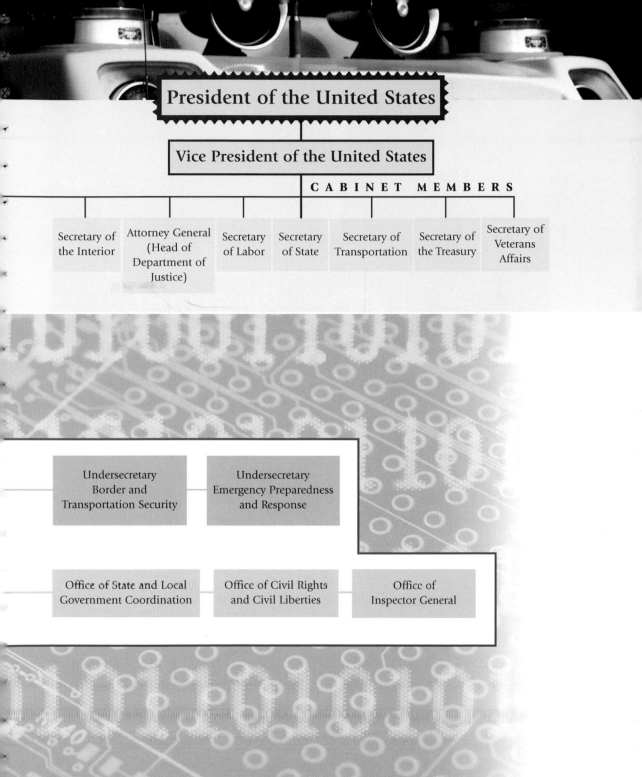

President of the United States

Vice President of the United States

CABINET MEMBERS

Secretary of the Interior	Attorney General (Head of Department of Justice)	Secretary of Labor	Secretary of State	Secretary of Transportation	Secretary of the Treasury	Secretary of Veterans Affairs

Undersecretary Border and Transportation Security	Undersecretary Emergency Preparedness and Response

Office of State and Local Government Coordination	Office of Civil Rights and Civil Liberties	Office of Inspector General

President George W. Bush signs the Homeland Security Appropriations Act of 2004 on October 1, 2003. The act provided the new Department of Homeland Security with $30 billion. Standing at far right is the department's first secretary, Tom Ridge.

Terrorism of this kind forced Americans to face these previously unimaginable and deeply frightening questions.

It now appears that with the amount of information the Federal Bureau of Investigation (FBI) and the Central Intelligence Agency (CIA)—the nation's two main intelligence-gathering agencies—had collected before September 11, more could and should have been done to prevent the horrific attacks. Both agencies possessed information that, if it had been shared, could have warned of the upcoming events and possibly prevented them. Since the attacks, there have been major investigations into what went wrong in the two intelligence agencies. The disorganized bureaucracy of the two agencies and a lack of communication between the two have been blamed for the failures.

Within two weeks of the attacks on the World Trade Center and the Pentagon, President George W. Bush announced the creation of the Office of Homeland Security under the leadership of Tom Ridge, former governor of Pennsylvania and a longtime friend of the president's. The new office was designed to protect the American public from another major terrorist attack. Initially, however, the office did little concrete work other than advising the president on domestic security issues. By November 2002, the office would be rethought, expanded, and turned into a new cabinet-level department of the government. This put it on an equal footing with other important cabinet offices, like the Departments of Defense, Agriculture, and Commerce.

The Department of Homeland Security was created with four specific purposes in mind: to reduce America's vulnerability to terrorism by controlling the nation's borders, to minimize the damage and speed the recovery from attacks that do occur, to develop antiterrorist technologies, and to review intelligence from all agencies of government. The department does not serve a brand-new purpose. There have always been government agencies working to defend the United States and its citizens from attacks at home and abroad. Rather, the new department brings together under one roof many agencies of the government that already exist, helping to create a more unified effort.

The terrorist attacks of September 11 highlighted the need for a reorganization of the U.S. government. However, before sweeping new powers could be granted to the U.S. government with which to fight terrorist threats, the often-troubled history of homeland security had to be reviewed. Striking the right balance between law and order on one side and freedoms and civil liberties on the other has been a debate that has raged since the times of the ancient Greeks. The playwright Sophocles and the philosopher Plato both pondered this very question, but no individual or government yet has come up with the perfect formula. American responses to domestic threats have often gone beyond the legal limits imposed on the government by the U.S. Constitution. Both private citizens and immigrants have occasionally been unjustly denied their guaranteed rights and freedoms during times of heightened national security. It is the very difficult job of the Department of Homeland Security to protect citizens from attack while also safeguarding their personal freedoms, the very freedoms upon which the United States was founded.

CHAPTER ONE

The History of Homeland Security

Before September 11, 2001, the United States had mostly remained free from attacks on its soil. This was mainly due to the fact that it was physically isolated from its enemies. The Pacific and Atlantic oceans separate the United States from Europe and Asia, which made any attacks extremely difficult, not to mention rare. The United States has also been fortunate to have two consistently friendly neighbors in Mexico and Canada, the only countries bordering American soil. Not since the nineteenth century has the threat of war on American soil been a concern. Even the Japanese bombing of Pearl Harbor in Hawaii on December 7, 1941, was a long-distance attack on a U.S. military installation on an island that is separated from the American mainland by more than 1,000 miles (1,609 kilometers) of ocean.

The Japanese attack on Pearl Harbor was the first foreign attack on American soil in more than a century. Fighting in the name of national security has more often been carried out in foreign lands, such as Vietnam and Korea. Wars in these two countries were fought as part of American foreign policy during the Cold War era, which called for combating Communism around the world. The Communist Soviet Union (modern-day Russia and various newly independent former Soviet republics) and its vast arsenal of nuclear bombs and missiles pointed at the United States posed an obvious threat to the nation. The United States tried to limit Soviet power and influence wherever possible without directly confronting the Soviets and prompting an all-out nuclear war.

A threat to national security usually comes from a specific group of people. For example, the September 11 hijackers were all Islamic radicals, and most of them were from Saudi Arabia. Because of this, specific groups are often targeted in the name of homeland security, which raises some difficult questions. What should the United States do with immigrants from hostile countries living within its borders? Do these people still have the rights guaranteed to American citizens in the Constitution? Or does the safety of the larger population merit taking away the rights of this smaller group? These are questions that the United States has faced every time that there has been a

On December 7, 1941, Japanese fighter pilots attacked the U.S. Pacific Fleet stationed at Pearl Harbor, Hawaii. The surprise raid left 2,403 American service people dead and badly damaged or destroyed 188 U.S. planes and 8 battleships. Within hours, President Franklin D. Roosevelt declared war on Japan.

threat to national security. American history demonstrates many interesting examples of how the government has responded to these questions.

Internment of Japanese Americans

During World War II, America found itself with what it perceived to be a major problem. At the time of the attack on Pearl Harbor and the United States' declaration of war against Japan, well over 100,000 Japanese Americans lived on the West Coast of the United States. President Franklin D. Roosevelt's administration, the U.S. Congress, and many American citizens feared that these Japanese Americans (many of whom were born in the United States and were full citizens) would remain more loyal to the land of their ancestry than to America. It was thought that they might actually be helping the Japanese cause in some secret way.

The possibility that these people might arm themselves in the name of Japan and attack the U.S. government was extremely unlikely. For the most part, these immigrants had escaped poverty and repression in Japan to find freedom and opportunity in America. The government, however, thought that the threat these immigrants posed to the country was too great of a risk. More than 120,000 Japanese Americans were forced out of their homes and interned—or imprisoned—in camps throughout the American West. For several years, they were not allowed to leave these barbed-wire compounds. When they were released after the war, new families were living in their homes and their businesses had long since gone bankrupt. The Japanese Americans were treated as if they had already committed treason and were forced to pay the price for it. The saddest part is that in most cases these people entered the camps feeling that they were showing their loyalty to their new home and nation. The rights of Japanese Americans were severely abused in the name of domestic security. To this day, Japanese internment remains one of the most shameful episodes in American history.

Japanese Americans from San Pedro, California, arrive at the Santa Anita Assembly Center on April 5, 1942. The detainees would live at this center— a former racetrack—until the government was ready to move them farther inland to one of the ten more permanent "relocation centers," or detention camps, in Colorado, Arizona, Wyoming, Idaho, and California.

Many people argue that increased homeland security always means that citizens must give up some of their rights and freedoms. Throughout American history this has often been the case. The groups suspected of anti-American activities are often composed of recent immigrants. All immigrants from these particular ethnic groups then become suspect, regardless of their political beliefs. Immigrants often are not yet allowed to vote and, therefore, have little influence with politicians and the government. They usually come to America for work because they cannot support their families in their own countries. They lack the money

THE DEPARTMENT OF HOMELAND SECURITY AT WORK: IMMIGRATION AND BORDERS

Pedestrians and drivers prepare to cross the U.S.-Mexican border into San Ysidro, California.

The Department of Homeland Security became responsible for administering the nation's immigration laws on March 1, 2003, when the Immigration and Naturalization Service (INS) became part of the department. Through the U.S. Citizenship and Immigration Services (USCIS), the department welcomes immigrants into the country, issuing work visas, reviewing applications for U.S. citizenship, and granting asylum to refugees. Immigration enforcement, which is the responsibility of the Directorate of Border and Transportation Security, includes preventing immigrants from entering the country unlawfully, finding and removing those who are living in the United States unlawfully, and preventing terrorists and other criminals from entering or living in the

United States. The Department of Homeland Security tries to strike a balance between welcoming law-abiding visitors and immigrants and identifying and keeping out possible terrorists. It tries to make certain that America continues to welcome visitors and those who seek opportunity within our shores while excluding terrorists and their supporters.

to hire lawyers or lobbyists to help defend themselves against attempts by the government to limit their rights and freedoms. This is what Japanese Americans faced in the 1940s. Many Arab Americans are now facing a similar situation.

Terrorism Reaches American Shores

Terrorism has long been a security concern for the United States, but it was not always its main concern. Until September 11, 2001, the majority of terrorist attacks directed against Americans occurred outside of the United States. In 1998, for example, Al Qaeda, the terrorist network responsible for the September 11 attacks, blew up the American embassies in Kenya and Tanzania, both in Africa. The bombings, which occurred within minutes of each other, killed 224 people, most of whom were Africans. In response, the president at the time,

17

Bill Clinton, fired several cruise missiles at Al Qaeda chief Osama bin Laden's training camps in Afghanistan. The missiles hit the camp but missed their real target—bin Laden. In 2000, bin Laden delivered his retaliation by bombing the USS *Cole* in a harbor in Yemen, killing seventeen sailors.

Terrorism has actually reached American soil a few times, however. In 1995, an anti-government American terrorist named Timothy McVeigh blew up a federal building in Oklahoma City, Oklahoma, killing 168 people. Another homegrown terrorist who plagued the United States in the 1980s and 1990s was the so-called Unabomber, Ted Kaczynski. The Unabomber was a mentally ill individual who developed a deep hatred of technology and lived in primitive solitude in rural Montana. To protest the modern world, he sent bombs by mail to scientists, academics, and executives of major corporations. Several people were killed by these mail bombs. Many others were severely injured. Another example of terrorism used as protest is found in the late 1960s and early 1970s, with a student group called the Weathermen. These American men and women turned to terrorist bombings when peaceful protests seemed to be doing nothing to bring about an end to the Vietnam War. Finally, the World Trade Center, destroyed by the September 11 attacks, was actually bombed eight years earlier, probably by Al Qaeda. That bombing resulted in six deaths but no major structural damage to the towers.

At top, rescue workers clear debris after the 1998 bombing of the U.S. Embassy in Nairobi, Kenya. At bottom, crews search for survivors in the rubble of the Murrah Federal Building in Oklahoma City, Oklahoma, in 1995. The building was destroyed in an attack by an American, Timothy McVeigh.

Despite these disturbing outbreaks of political violence on American soil, terrorism was never the government's top homeland security priority until September 11, 2001. By successfully attacking the Pentagon and World Trade Center, terrorists demonstrated their ability to strike at the financial and political heart of the nation with devastating effect. Following the end of the Cold War and the new age of terror ushered in on September 11, the major security threat to Americans was no longer long-range Soviet missiles. Instead, less easily detected and monitored weapons like box cutters, hijacked commercial planes, mail bombs, poisoned water and food, and "dirty bombs" (crude nuclear devices that could spread deadly radiation over a limited area) became the most feared threats. America's intelligence agencies had to adapt to this new reality.

The CIA and FBI

The CIA has long been responsible for gathering intelligence about the threats posed by enemy governments. Today, it must also collect all the information available on the plots being hatched by terrorist groups, which are far harder to track and eavesdrop on than are conventional governments. The CIA was founded during World War II and was known as the Office of Strategic Services (OSS). The OSS operated worldwide during the war. Its agents gathered intelligence behind enemy lines, as well as far away from the fighting.

They did everything from sabotaging enemy positions to coordinating with resistance groups in occupied countries. After the war, it was obvious that such a foreign intelligence agency was still needed. Since the OSS was created during wartime, however, it needed to be reorganized for peacetime operations. The CIA was the result.

During the Cold War years, the CIA's powers were often abused in the name of national security. The CIA was responsible for a number of questionable decisions, including the toppling of governments the U.S. government disagreed with, the setting up of violent dictators it did agree with, and many assassinations of political enemies. Some of its actions were illegal, and Congress had to hold hearings on its secret activities more than once to figure out how to rein in the agency. However, the CIA was also responsible for keeping the nation safe from attack during an extremely dangerous period of intense hostility with the Soviet Union. This was by no means an easy job, and the CIA deserves all due credit for this success. The often questionable means by which the agency secured America's safety during the Cold War are still being debated today, even as the CIA begins to target the new enemy—international terrorists. The same question of how far the United States should go to protect its citizens and way of life is again being asked, and the answers are not any clearer now than they were several decades ago.

The FBI is the CIA's domestic counterpart. It, too, is responsible for gathering intelligence on threats to national security, but it does so within the United States rather than abroad. President Theodore Roosevelt planted the seeds of the bureau in 1908. The need for a federal law enforcement agency arose because of the biased, political nature of law enforcement that existed throughout the nineteenth century. Those who had enough money or connections could often break the law without penalty. The creation of the FBI was supposed to put an end to this corruption while also allowing the U.S. government to enforce the laws of the nation across state lines. In this sense, the FBI was like a federal police force.

The FBI has been responsible for a large number of tasks since its creation, from chasing bank robbers and drug dealers to catching business executives and investment bankers who break financial rules and steal money. Like the CIA, however, the FBI has not always done the right thing while fighting its enemies. In the 1950s and 1960s, the FBI gathered information on and harassed peaceful political groups—such as student groups, civil rights groups, and labor unions—throughout the United States simply because it believed these groups to be threats to national security. In reality, these groups were exercising their democratic right to protest what they believed were unfair domestic and global situations.

The FBI is now the most important law enforcement agency combating terrorism within the nation's borders.

National Guard troops patrol Los Angeles International Airport on March 27, 2003, during an orange-level alert. When the Department of Homeland Security raises the terrorist threat level to orange, it means that there is a high risk of terrorist attacks. During an orange alert, National Guard troops can be called in to help federal, state, and local law enforcement agencies with their security efforts.

In October 2001, it gained even more power when Congress passed the USA Patriot Act. This act allows the government to access private information on citizens by, for example, making it easier for the government to tap people's phones or bug their offices and homes. The law also allows the U.S. authorities to hold illegal immigrants in custody without a trial. Many people have criticized the act for giving the government too much power and access to private information.

A Coordinated Approach

The Department of Homeland Security relies upon the intelligence gathered by the FBI and CIA to protect American soil, but it is not itself a law enforcement or spy agency. Instead, the department is designed to prevent terrorist attacks by improving domestic security and, in the event of an attack, respond quickly and effectively. If the FBI and CIA are at the forefront of the war against terror, the Department of Homeland Security and the various groups included within it play very important supporting roles, such as patrolling the nation's waterways and airports, carefully screening all visitors and temporary residents of the United States, and, if worse comes to worst, providing disaster relief.

Many of the agencies now included in the Department of Homeland Security have had long, complicated histories of their own. For example, the Federal Emergency Management Agency (FEMA) has been responsible for responding to disasters (both natural and human-made) within the United States since 1979. The idea of disaster relief first came about in 1806, and since then, the responsibility has been passed down through the hands of the Reconstruction Finance Corporation and the Army Corps of Engineers.

The Coast Guard has been responsible for protecting the nation's harbors and shores for many years. It was created by Congress in 1789 to enforce tariffs (taxes on traded goods) and build and maintain lighthouses. All of the Coast Guard's current duties were consolidated in 1939. More recently, the Coast Guard's main concerns have been intercepting drug smugglers and illegal immigrants. Today, it has the huge responsibility of securing our thousands of miles of shoreline and hundreds of ports from any potential terrorist attacks.

As part of Operation Liberty Shield, a U.S. Coast Guard boat *(foreground)* patrols New York Harbor with a boat from the New York Police Department Harbor Unit. The operation is a national program designed to ensure the safety of the nation's ports and waterways through the cooperation of local, state, and federal law enforcement and security agencies.

While millions of people enter the United States every year by air, hundreds of thousands of tons of cargo enter the country every year by sea. The ease with which a nuclear, biological, or chemical weapon could be smuggled into an ordinary shipping container is a huge concern. It would be impossible to inspect every container for illegal weapons or substances, so new systems need to be developed to ensure the safety of these important goods. The Coast Guard—working with officials from many other government departments and agencies—will be at the center of this effort.

CHAPTER TWO

Important Figures in Homeland Security

Homeland security is an idea that has meant many different things to many different people. For George Washington and the forefathers of the American government, it meant defending the borders against the English. For Abraham Lincoln, it meant defending the country against those in the South who wanted to secede and break the country into two over the issue of slavery. And until World War II, homeland security was simply not a major concern because few countries posed any threat to the distant and geographically isolated United States.

During World War II, however, homeland security became a major concern. The attack on Pearl Harbor killed more than

2,000 Americans and destroyed much of the navy's Pacific Fleet. The Nazis' rapid occupation of large portions of Europe was also an ominous sign of the future. It proved that a nation's borders could be moved—or erased—overnight. After the war, the Soviet Union—with its long-range nuclear missiles and sophisticated bombers, jets, and submarines—became a threat like no other nation had ever been before. America's sudden sense of vulnerability after Pearl Harbor and at the dawn of the nuclear age prompted many anxious calls for greater domestic security.

Joseph McCarthy

One of the people who rang the loudest alarms about domestic security was Wisconsin senator Joseph McCarthy. He believed that a group of communist sympathizers was operating within the government. He began a series of hearings designed to root out communists in the State Department and in different branches of the military. In reality, McCarthy was targeting innocent citizens whose political beliefs were more liberal than his but still firmly democratic and patriotic. Many people's lives were ruined by his accusations of communist sympathies. They were often black-listed, which meant no one would hire them or work with them.

Over time, more and more people began to doubt the truth of Senator McCarthy's accusations. His last shred of credibility was lost when he accused the U.S. Army of harboring communists. This angered President Dwight D. Eisenhower, a former

On February 9, 1950, Joseph McCarthy *(foreground, right)*, a Republican senator from Wisconsin, claimed that he had a list of 205 State Department employees who were communists. While he offered little proof, the senator damaged many reputations and frightened many of his political opponents.

general, and Congress turned its back on McCarthy. His influence quickly diminished. In the end, McCarthy's false accusations were another black eye on the U.S. government's record of protecting its citizens' rights. Unproven claims were once again taken as fact when the public felt threatened. Constitutional protections and the right of due process—the right to a fair trial—had been ignored in the name of homeland security.

J. Edgar Hoover

Another important figure in the history of domestic security is J. Edgar Hoover. He became the head of the FBI in 1924 and quickly turned it into the national law enforcement agency it is today. He fired those in the department who had been given jobs through connections or did not meet his strict requirements for agents. In the 1930s, the agency gained national attention under Hoover for aggressively taking on organized crime. During World War II, the FBI led all intelligence operations within the nation's borders. After the war, the bureau continued to direct all domestic intelligence gathering and began running background checks on all federal employees in an attempt to prevent foreign agents from entering the government.

As time passed, however, Hoover took his powers within the FBI too far. A fearful and controlling man, he spied and kept files on any American he felt was either a threat to him personally or to the nation. Never before had the U.S. government violated civil liberties so recklessly in order to look into the private lives of citizens. Hoover showed his worst side when it came to the civil rights movement. He continually tried to question the integrity and morals of the Reverend Martin Luther King Jr. In order to try to squash growing sympathy among white Americans for King and the civil rights movement, Hoover even withheld evidence in the trial of several Ku Klux Klan members who, in 1963, had firebombed a church in Birmingham, Alabama, killing four young girls.

Because of the hysteria surrounding the Cold War competition with the Soviet Union and the high-stakes game of the nuclear arms race, Hoover was given enormous power to interfere

THE DEPARTMENT OF HOMELAND SECURITY AT WORK: RESEARCH AND TECHNOLOGY

In order to develop the tools and techniques necessary to combat terrorists and their destructive weapons, the Department of Homeland Security is trying to bring together the latest technology and most talented American scientists. The department's Science and Technology Directorate is responsible for researching and organizing the scientific, engineering, and technological resources of the United States and harnessing them to develop high-tech tools that will help protect the homeland. Universities, the private sector, and federal laboratories will all be involved in these research and development efforts. The Homeland Security Advanced Research Projects Agency is designed to get an early jump on this research and quickly provide some tools to help fill gaps in homeland defenses.

in the lives of Americans. Whether or not he really believed that spying on Americans and trying to ruin Dr. King's reputation served the interests of national security, he knew that he could get away with it because few were brave enough to take on the FBI in such a political climate. It was too easy to be branded a traitor or a communist and have one's life ruined as a result.

30

An SS-19 strategic missile warhead is loaded into a missile silo near Saratov, Russia. During the Cold War as many as 300 SS-19 missiles were stationed in the Soviet Union. Because these missiles could carry nuclear warheads, the United States and its allies lived in fear of the Soviet Union's intentions, creating the anti-communist climate that people like Senator Joseph McCarthy and FBI director J. Edgar Hoover thrived on.

Tom Ridge

There have been many important individuals in the history of domestic security, but Tom Ridge was the first secretary of Homeland Security. He was born in Munhall, Pennsylvania, raised in nearby Erie, and later attended Harvard University. While in law school, he was drafted to serve in the Vietnam War. After serving with distinction, Ridge returned to the United States to finish his law degree.

After working as a successful defense lawyer for almost twenty years, Tom Ridge decided to enter politics in 1982, the year he was elected to Congress. He worked his way up the political ladder and in 1994 became governor of Pennsylvania. Toward the end of his second and final term as governor,

Michael Chertoff *(far right)* is sworn in as the secretary of Homeland Security on March 3, 2005, in Washington, D.C. He was only the second person in the nation's history to head the office. Holding the Bible is his wife, Meryl Justin. President George W. Bush *(far left)* looks on while Supreme Court justice Sandra Day O'Connor *(second from left)* swears Chertoff in.

Ridge began looking for a new job. As George W. Bush's 2000 presidential campaign picked up steam, Tom Ridge's name began to be discussed as a potential candidate for vice president.

Ultimately, President Bush selected Dick Cheney, former secretary of defense, as his running mate. However, he did not forget his longtime friend from Pennsylvania. When the Office of Homeland Security was created in the aftermath of the September 11 terror attacks, President Bush chose Tom Ridge as its director.

Ridge's name was chosen from a short list of candidates because President Bush felt his leadership and motivational skills would be an invaluable asset in reorganizing the government's domestic security apparatus and making Americans feel safe again.

Ridge's first job as secretary of Homeland Security was the very complicated task of figuring out how to fold 22 different agencies and 170,000 federal employees into a single, unified, brand-new government department.

Michael Chertoff

On March 3, 2005, Michael Chertoff was sworn in as the secretary of Homeland Security at the beginning of George W. Bush's second term as U.S. president. Chertoff was only the second Homeland Security chief in the nation's history. The son of a rabbi, Chertoff grew up in Elizabeth, New Jersey, attended Harvard University, and went on to become a federal prosecutor, assistant U.S. Attorney General, and U.S. Court of Appeals judge. While his nomination was confirmed with a unanimous vote in the U.S. Senate, it did generate some controversy. As one of Bush's chief advisers on legal strategies relating to the War on Terror—particularly the policy on the detainment of Middle Eastern immigrants—Chertoff alienated some liberal Democrats and many citizens concerned about the possible erosion of Americans' civil liberties.

CHAPTER THREE

How the Department of Homeland Security Works

When President George W. Bush announced the creation of the new Department of Homeland Security on June 6, 2002, he outlined its four-part mission (see page 9). Creating the department out of twenty-two existing agencies was the most massive reorganization of the U.S. government since 1947. In that year, the Department of War and the Department of the Navy were merged to create the Department of Defense, bringing all the nation's defense agencies under one roof.

When the Department of Homeland Security was created, many different government groups and agencies had to be folded into the homeland security organization. In fact, in its first two years of existence, the majority of the department's time and effort was spent on figuring out how to incorporate 170,000 employees and 22 agencies that had rarely worked together into one smoothly functioning department. On March 1, 2003, all of these agencies were officially transferred into the Department of Homeland Security.

The Department of Homeland Security is composed of four subgroups. They are Information Analysis and Infrastructure Protection; Science and Technology; Border and Transportation Security; and Emergency Preparedness and Response. Together, these divisions share an enormous variety of responsibilities and perform a wide range of activities.

Information Analysis and Infrastructure Protection

The September 11 attacks exposed the most important failing of the nation's security system: its inability to use the intelligence that it had gathered about terrorist threats in a way that would help prevent attacks. Early in the process that led to the creation of the Department of Homeland Security, many people were calling for the FBI and the CIA to form the central core of the new department. In this proposed arrangement, the two intelligence agencies would have focused their efforts on detecting terrorist threats at home and abroad and shared their information. They would have been able to use one another's intelligence to detect threats that might otherwise slip through the cracks.

In the end, though, President Bush decided not to include the two intelligence agencies within the new department. White House planners finally decided that making these two agencies part of the Department of Homeland Security would have made it more difficult for them to complete their other duties. The FBI is responsible for many federal crimes that have nothing to do with terrorism, such as bank robberies and money laundering. Similarly, the CIA is responsible for intelligence gathering around the world, much of which is not related to terrorism.

Instead, an intelligence-sharing scheme was devised that is supposed to provide the Department of Homeland Security with all of the intelligence that it needs. Through its Office of Information Analysis and Infrastructure Protection, the department will receive summary reports from the two agencies. These reports help the department determine the general level of danger posed by terrorists at any given time. The level of danger is announced to the public in the form of the department's color-coded warning system. In colors ranging from green (low risk) to red (severe risk), five different threat levels let Americans know the amount of caution they should use as they go about their daily lives.

Another essential mission of the department's Office of Information Analysis and Infrastructure Protection is to study the vulnerability of potential targets within the United States and the likelihood of attacks against them. Across the country, there are

The Homeland Security Advisory System *(right)* is a color-coded warning chart that indicates various levels of terrorist threat. The lowest level of threat is green and indicates that the risk of a terror attack in the near future is low. The United States has not been below yellow ("elevated") since the system was introduced on March 12, 2002, in the wake of the September 11, 2001, attacks.

Homeland Security Advisory System

SEVERE
Severe Risk of Terrorist Attacks

HIGH
High Risk of Terrorist Attacks

ELEVATED
Significant Risk of Terrorist Attacks

GUARDED
General Risk of Terrorist Attacks

LOW
Low Risk of Terrorist Attacks

thousands of potential targets for terrorist attacks. Because terrorism relies on surprise, future terrorist attacks will probably be much different from anything that has been seen before. This leaves the nation's infrastructure—its buildings, roads, railways, power plants, reservoirs, tunnels, and bridges—very vulnerable to terrorist attacks.

Nuclear power plants have caused the most fear in this regard. A plane flown into a nuclear plant, or a bomb placed inside one, could lead to an explosion that would spread high levels of radiation across a wide area, sickening and killing thousands of people. The destruction of a dam and the resulting flooding could destroy thousands of homes and businesses, make many families homeless, and lead to enormous loss of life. The destruction of key parts of the nation's power grid—which

Many Americans worry that nuclear power plants could be the next target of terrorists. A terrorist attack upon a nuclear plant like the one shown above might trigger an explosive meltdown that could kill millions of people in the surrounding area, spread radiation for hundreds of miles, and cause deadly health problems for years to come.

supplies us with electricity and powers most of our machines—could cripple large sections of the country. The effects of a major power loss were seen in the summer of 2003 when a series of power line failures led to a blackout throughout large swaths of the Northeast and Midwest.

There are many possible terrorist targets across the country that were not designed with terrorism in mind. They were not built to withstand the impact of a commercial airliner or a large truck bomb, so their security is of the utmost importance. The Office of Information Analysis and Infrastructure Protection is responsible for figuring out how vulnerable these sites are and what can be done to make them safer. There are so many different potential targets, and so many different possible ways to attack them, that, in reality, they can never be made 100 percent safe from attack. But it is this office's job to figure out which are the most at risk and how disastrous the consequences of an attack would be.

Science and Technology

The department's Office of Science and Technology is an extremely important part of the overall homeland security strategy. Its main responsibility is to prepare for biological, chemical, or nuclear attacks. It must develop strategies to respond to any of these types of attacks if they do occur. It is also responsible for developing methods to monitor and prevent the smuggling of such weapons into the United States. To fulfill both these goals, the office conducts a lot of research. This research includes finding vaccines to fight the effects of biological and chemical weapons; preparing hospitals to be able to treat victims of biological, chemical, or nuclear attacks; and developing technology that can detect these types of weapons at our borders.

The technology side of the Science and Technology Office works to develop new ways of responding to terrorism. It seeks to develop new devices that can detect weapons of mass destruction at our borders as well as equipment that can halt or lessen the damage of a biological, chemical, or nuclear attack. The number of technological breakthroughs that are sure to follow in the coming years will be impressive. Many independent businesses, funded in part by the Department of Homeland Security, are already addressing the security failures that allowed the September 11 terrorist attacks to happen, as well as the equipment failures that made the response to the attacks ineffective. For example, one company has already designed vehicles equipped to communicate with any type of radio. If these vehicles had been in use on September 11, 2001, hundreds of firefighters who were killed in the World Trade Center when their faulty radio system took too long to relay evacuation orders might still be alive today. Another company has designed a small scanner that can tell if a passport or driver's license is authentic so that known terrorists cannot use fake identification.

Border and Transportation Security

Another extremely important job of the Department of Homeland Security is its role in border and transportation security. All of the September 11 hijackers entered the country in the two years before the attacks. Most of them entered only months before. The borders of the United States are vast. The two shared with Canada and Mexico are a combined 6,500 miles (10,461 km) long. Furthermore, 500 million people enter and leave the United States every year. There are so many different points of entry along these borders and at the nation's hundreds of international airports and seaports that policing this enormous territory is an extremely difficult and challenging job.

It is not surprising then that the Border and Transportation Security Office will be the largest of the four offices in the department. Transferred into this office were the Customs Service (which regulates the importing of goods), the Immigration and Naturalization Service (INS), the Transportation Security Administration (TSA), and a long list of organizations that provide support. Furthermore, Customs and part of the INS were collapsed into one organization called Customs and Border Protection (CBP). Another part of the INS, renamed the U.S. Citizenship and Immigration Services (USCIS), now handles all the paperwork related to immigration. The new Bureau of Immigration and Customs enforcement is responsible for law enforcement related to immigration.

One of the newest initiatives of the Border and Transportation Security Office is the U.S.-VISIT program. With this program, the nation's borders will quickly become more organized. Many of the September 11 hijackers were living in the country on expired visas. If the INS had been keeping better track of them, these men may have been sent back to their home countries before they had a chance to go through with their plan.

Immigrants wait in line to apply for visas outside the Immigration and Naturalization Service (INS) building in Los Angeles, California. In 2003, the INS became the U.S. Citizenship and Immigration Services (USCIS), operating under the Department of Homeland Security. The USCIS took over many of the former INS' immigration-related duties.

Now, when foreign citizens enter the country, they will be kept track of from the minute they apply for a visa until the moment they leave the country. At the borders, they will be electronically fingerprinted and photographed so that border officers can match up the person leaving the country with the name they have on their computer screen. All official actions, such as hospital visits and appointments at immigration offices within the United States, will be kept track of as well. Furthermore, the department will also try to keep track of the other countries that these travelers have visited. If they have

Foreigners arriving at U.S.-VISIT-capable airports and seaports now have their index fingers scanned and a digital photo of their faces taken. This information is stored in a database, along with the person's visa number, and compared against watch lists of known terrorists and criminals. At right, a visitor arriving at Hartsfield-Jackson International Airport in Atlanta, Georgia, has his finger scanned.

visited countries known to be terrorist havens, their applications for entry into the United States will receive closer attention. The idea behind the program is to gather as much information as possible about an individual attempting to enter the country in order to make an educated decision about whether that person should be allowed in.

Emergency Preparedness and Response

The Office of Emergency Preparedness and Response is the fourth office within the Department of Homeland Security. It is concerned with the "first responders"—the police officers, firefighters, and emergency medical personnel who are the first people to respond to any disaster. The events of

September 11 showed how important it is to be prepared to respond to terrorist attacks. The New York City Fire Department was not ready to deal with a disaster of that type or magnitude. The firefighter's instructions had to be radioed from the fire chief through each individual firehouse's radio system. The time lag that this caused doomed many firefighters in the World Trade Center. When it became clear that the towers were about to collapse, evacuation orders were sent out but did not reach many firefighters in time.

If the next terrorist attack involves a biological or chemical weapon or the detonation of a nuclear device, the need to be prepared for rapid response will be even more critical. The first responders will have to know exactly how to deal with any medical issues if they are to save victims' lives and limit any further damage. Understanding this need, the Office of Emergency Preparedness and Response trains first responders all across the country and provides the money needed to bring police and fire departments, hospitals, and their equipment up to code. A government agency with more than twenty years of experience with emergency and disaster response—the Federal Emergency Management Agency (FEMA)—has been folded into the Office of Emergency Preparedness and Response. FEMA will continue to be the first federal organization to arrive at the scene of every type of disaster, from terrorist attacks and train wrecks to wildfires

THE DEPARTMENT OF HOMELAND SECURITY AT WORK: THREATS AND SECURITY

When the Department of Homeland Security was created in 2002, the Secret Service—the agency devoted to protecting the president, vice president, their families, and visiting foreign leaders—became a part of this new department. In

Mounted U.S. Park Police officers patrol outside the White House.

order to protect the president, the Secret Service seeks help from other federal, state, and local law enforcement agencies. For example, when the president is working at the White House, the Secret Service Uniformed Division, the Washington Metropolitan Police Department, and the U.S. Park Police patrol the streets and parks nearby to prevent any unwanted intruders from gaining access to the White House grounds. When the president travels away from Washington, a team of Secret Service agents arrives several days earlier and works with the host city and state law enforcement and public safety officials to jointly establish the security measures needed to protect the president.

Two officials from the Federal Emergency Management Agency (FEMA) fly in a helicopter over the Rappahannock River in Virginia in September 2003. They are surveying the damage left behind by Hurricane Isabel, which passed through the area the previous day.

and floods. It responds to disasters by providing information and advice to local officials. Perhaps more important, FEMA also brings supplies and money to aid in disaster relief and recovery.

CHAPTER FOUR

The Future of Homeland Security

T he Department of Homeland Security is a work in progress. Its creation required a major reorganization of the government. As enemy threats change over time, the department's structure and mission will probably evolve, too. Some agencies will prove to be less important in securing the homeland and be closed down, while others will prove to be absolutely essential and be beefed up. Agencies now outside the department may be incorporated into the Department of Homeland Security in an ongoing attempt to consolidate security efforts. The list of agencies now part of the department is, therefore, likely to change in the future.

An Uncertain Future

Right now, the Department of Homeland Security is geared toward preventing another major terrorist attack in the United States. If more attacks fail to occur and the threat level seems to decrease, the department may start to play a larger role as a disaster relief organization, through FEMA. The prevention of terrorism—the very reason for its creation—may someday become just a footnote to the department's history. As the long history of homeland security has taught us, threats to Americans and to the country are constantly changing. What seems to be a dire threat today may seem insignificant and overblown tomorrow. However, until the day arrives when Americans truly feel free of the deadly reach of terrorism, the Department of Homeland Security will continue to focus on the prevention of further terrorist attacks on the nation and its people.

Future attacks and intelligence will force the department to rethink and redefine its operations time and time again. No one really knows what to expect when it comes to the future of terrorism. All anyone knows is that the unexpected should be expected. This makes the future of the Department of Homeland Security extremely difficult to predict. What can be said for certain is that the department will attempt to prepare itself, the government, local law enforcement, and average citizens for any type of attack that seems possible or likely.

Spent fuel rods are stored underwater at the Savannah River storage site in Aiken, South Carolina. To help prevent the spread of bomb-grade nuclear material, the U.S. government has decided to melt down these fuel rods and mix them with nonreactive substances, forming harmless metal bricks that can be safely stored in permanent storage facilities.

While the September 11 attacks were truly horrific, future attacks may be even more terrifying and destructive. Terrorist attacks featuring deadly weapons—chemical, biological, or nuclear—could be even more devastating and deadly than anything we have seen so far. It is difficult to understand how the government can possibly prepare for the wide range of weapons and strategies terrorists might use against us. It has been reported that for nearly a decade Osama bin Laden, the leader of Al Qaeda, has been actively seeking the ingredients needed to build a nuclear weapon. Because of the killing power of radiation, it is extremely important to disrupt any planned nuclear attack before it is carried out. More than 100,000 people died in the only two atomic strikes ever directed at human populations—the U.S. bombing of the Japanese cities Hiroshima and Nagasaki in 1945. The weapons have only become more deadly in the more than fifty years since those attacks. While biological and chemical weapon attacks promise less extensive damage and death than nuclear attacks, they still have the capability to kill many hundreds, if not thousands, of people at one time.

The Perils of Technology

Another aspect of national security that will become more and more important in the future is technology. When the Department of Homeland Security was created, the Secret Service was included in its roster. This was mainly because the Secret Service deals with computer crimes in addition to its better-known duty of protecting the president, vice president, their families, and visiting foreign leaders. The types of terrorism that we are familiar with today—hijackings, bombings, hostage taking—may someday become too well defended against to be effective for terrorists. Cyber-terrorism has been one of the forms of attack that government officials have often mentioned as a concern for the future.

Because almost 3,000 people died extremely violent deaths on September 11, 2001, the possibility of cyber-terrorism does not seem very frightening in comparison. Computers being

THE DEPARTMENT OF HOMELAND SECURITY AT WORK: EMERGENCIES AND DISASTERS

In 2003, the Department of Homeland Security announced the award of nearly $400 million to ten states to help improve the response and preparedness capabilities of their first responders. The department has made available more than $4.4 billion in funding for similar grants since March 1, 2003. Through the Department of Homeland Security's Emergency Preparedness and Response Directorate, $165 million in grants has been awarded to help state and local governments become better prepared for a wide range of emergencies—including natural disasters, industrial accidents, and terrorist attacks— and improve their emergency management techniques.

Emergency workers in biohazard suits participate in a mock drill in Seattle, Washington. The drill was designed to simulate the effects of a terrorist nuclear attack.

infected by a virus and "crashing" does not seem to qualify as terrorism when planes and buildings full of innocent people have actually crashed down around us. However, if a hostile group really wants to disrupt the American way of life, a powerful computer virus is just as capable of causing crippling damage as any massive explosion. Work and play are central ways of life in the United States, and both rely heavily on cyberspace and sharing information by computer. Furthermore, much of the United States' defense and electrical systems rely on computer programs and network communications.

As time passes, the nation will only become more "wired" and dependent upon computer technology. Unfortunately, a computer network's infrastructure—its operating system, information storage, and programming—are as fragile and easily destroyed as the infrastructure of any city. Like a city, computer networks are simply a system of bridges, tunnels, roads, storage facilities, and power centers. A single powerful virus, spreading via e-mail like wildfire, can destroy these fragile connections. As the Department of Homeland Security reduces the risk of conventional terrorist attacks on American soil by tightening our nation's borders, screening out suspicious travelers, and inspecting incoming cargo, it can also be expected to pay closer attention to cyber-terrorism. After all, a terrorist does not need a visa or a plane ticket to wreak havoc in cyberspace.

Conclusion

T he need for a Department of Homeland Security was made perfectly clear on the morning of September 11, 2001. A long chain of mistakes and oversights allowed the attacks to occur and made response to them difficult. A murderous plan that took advantage of the United States' open borders and lax immigration enforcement had been perfectly executed. The hijackers had made it past immigration services, and once they were in the country, the INS had lost track of them. These men were able to carry box cutters aboard planes and use them as weapons. No air force planes were able to get in the air quickly enough to affect the outcome, even after the terrorists' intentions were understood. The intelligence system of the

United States had also been caught sleeping. As a result, nearly 3,000 people lost their lives in the wreckage of four commercial airplanes, the Pentagon, and the collapsed World Trade Center. The response to the disaster was understandably chaotic. The New York City Fire and Police departments were neither prepared nor equipped for a disaster of this scale. In the wake of these missteps, the need for a reorganization of much of the government was clear.

It is widely believed that the Department of Homeland Security is absolutely crucial for America's safety. Its duties are not new. The duties of domestic security have been performed by various government agencies—many of them now included in the Department of Homeland Security—since well before the department was created. Rethinking the priorities and procedures of these agencies was a necessary step after terrorists showed the enormous damage they could inflict on a poorly defended nation. But the Department of Homeland Security is only a part of the larger struggle to protect the United States against attacks at home and abroad, and it cannot provide the whole solution. A strong military, an efficient intelligence system, and an effective diplomatic corps are also large pieces of the puzzle.

The American public should feel more secure now than they did before the creation of the department. The threat warning system and greater security at airports are highly visible signs that the department is doing its job. The department's most valuable

Members of the National Guard patrol Chicago's O'Hare International Airport in 2001. Since the attacks of September 11, the Guard has been called on to help local and federal law enforcement agencies protect the nation's infrastructure (such as bridges, tunnels, and airports); help detect the possible use of chemical, biological, or nuclear weapons; and guard sensitive military bases and labs.

work occurs behind the scenes, however. It will be the small, unheralded actions that the department takes that will make our daily lives safer. The Department of Homeland Security is more of a supporting organization in the fight against terrorism than it is an active defender. Its full capabilities will only be seen if another attack does occur, and only then will we know its true value.

The ultimate test of the department's success will be how essential it seems to our daily lives sometime in the future. If the department's goals are met, the Department of Homeland Security will one day seem irrelevant, simply because it has done its job so well and the threat of terror seems to recede. If all becomes quiet on the terrorism front, we will know that the department has done its part in defending U.S. soil from enemy attacks.

September 11, 2001	Terrorists hijack four airplanes. Two of the planes are flown into the World Trade Center, in New York City; one is flown into the Pentagon building near Washington, D.C.; and the fourth crashes in a Pennsylvania field. Almost 3,000 people are killed, most of them in the collapse of the World Trade Center.
September 20, 2001	President Bush establishes the Office of Homeland Security, which will advise the president on security matters. Pennsylvania governor Tom Ridge is named to head the office.
October 26, 2001	President Bush signs the USA Patriot Act.
November 19, 2001	The Transportation Security Administration is created to address problems in airport security.
June 6, 2002	President Bush proposes the creation of the cabinet-level Department of Homeland Security. Tom Ridge will become the department's first secretary.
January 24, 2003–February 1, 2005	Tom Ridge
March 1, 2003	The last of the agencies to be transferred into the Department of Homeland Security are integrated, and the department becomes a fully functioning agency for the first time.

| May 12, 2003 | The first national homeland security drill—TopOff II—is run. |

| April 28, 2004 | George W. Bush issues a presidential directive instructing federal departments and agencies to find better ways to secure America from biological attacks. |

| May 20, 2004 | The DHS issues Security Directives requiring passenger train operators to better protect commuter, transit, and inter-city rail passengers from terrorist attacks. |

| June 21, 2004 | Secretary Tom Ridge announces new security measures to better protect the security of American ports. |

| August 25, 2004 | The DHS announces the awarding of contracts for the development and testing of a system that will protect commercial aircraft from shoulder-fired missiles. |

| March 3, 2005– | **Michael Chertoff** |

| March 3, 2005 | At the swearing-in ceremony for new Secretary of Homeland Security Michael Chertoff, President George W. Bush reasserts the department's commitment to guard the borders, strengthen airport and seaport security, institute better visa screening, and protect the nation's critical infrastructure from attack. He also discusses increasing cooperation between federal, state, and local law enforcement authorities and the training and equipping of state and local first responders to attack. |

bill A draft of a law presented to a legislature and submitted to a vote.

cabinet A council of the chief advisers to a head of state.

cabinet-level department A government office headed by a key adviser to a head of state, such as the president of the United States.

civil rights The legal rights of a citizen, protecting him or her from the oppression or injustice of government and individuals.

federal Of or relating to the central governing authority in a nation made up of several states or territories.

grant A payment by the government to a private business or individual for research.

immigrants Citizens or residents who have come from a foreign country.

import To bring into one's country something from another country.

infrastructure The support system of a city or country that allows it to function, such as the sanitation system, power plants, water pipelines, bridges, tunnels, highways, and railways.

initiative A new course of action.

intelligence Information about a threat or enemy.

smuggle To sneak illegal items or persons through the borders of a nation.

terrorism The act of attacking a group of innocent people in order to cause fear and death, often carried out to gain attention for a small group's cause or belief.

FOR MORE INFORMATION

Central Intelligence Agency
  Office of Public Affairs
Washington, DC 20505
Web site: http://www.cia.gov

Federal Bureau of Investigation
  J. Edgar Hoover Building
935 Pennsylvania Avenue NW
Washington, DC 20535
Web site: http://www.fbi.gov

Homeland Security—The
  White House
1600 Pennsylvania Avenue NW
Washington, DC 20500
Web site: http://www.whitehouse.
  gov/homeland

U.S. Department of Homeland
  Security
Washington, DC 20528
Web site: http://www.dhs.gov/
  dhspublic/index.jsp

U.S. Department of Justice
950 Pennsylvania Avenue NW
Washington, DC 20530
Web site: http://www.usdoj.gov

U.S. Department of Transportation
  Transportation Security
  Administration
TSA-6/400 7th Street SW
Washington, DC 20590
Web site: http://www.tsa.gov/public

WEB SITES

Due to the changing nature of
Internet links, the Rosen Publishing
Group, Inc., has developed an
online list of Web sites related to
the subject of this book. This site is
updated regularly. Please use this
link to access the list:

http://www.rosenlinks.com/tyg/hose

Gottfried, Ted. *Homeland Security Versus Constitutional Rights.* Washington, DC: 21st Century Books, 2003.

Hamilton, John. *Operation Noble Eagle, Vol. 9.* Edina, MN: ABDO Publishing Company, 2002.

Hampton, Wilborn. *September 11, 2001: Attack on New York City: Interviews and Accounts.* Cambridge, MA: Candlewick Press, 2003.

Horn, Geoffrey M. *The Cabinet and Federal Agencies.* Milwaukee, WI: Gareth Stevens Publishers, 2003.

Keely, Jennifer. *Deterring and Investigating Attack: The Role of the FBI and CIA.* San Diego, CA: Lucent Books, 2003.

Kerrigan, Michael. *The Department of Homeland Security.* Brookshire, TX: Mason Crest Publishers, 2002.

Meltzer, Milton. *The Day the Sky Fell: A History of Terrorism.* New York, NY: Random House Books for Young Readers, 2002.

Sanna, Ellyn. *Homeland Security Officer.* Brookshire, TX: Mason Crest Publishers, 2002.

Schaffer, Donna, and Alfred Meyer. *Secretary of Homeland Security.* Farmington Hills, MI: Gale Group, 2003.

Stewart, Gail B. *Defending the Borders: The Role of Border and Immigration Control.* San Diego, CA: Lucent Books, 2003.

Broder, David S. "Why Is This Man Smiling?" *Pittsburgh Post-Gazette*, December 2, 2002.

Davila, Florangela. "INS Sheds Its Name at Midnight: Agency to Be Under Homeland Umbrella." *Seattle Times*, February 28, 2003.

Eggen, Dan, and Dana Priest. "Intelligence Powers Set for New Agency; Department Would Shape Response to Threats." *Washington Post*, June 8, 2002.

"History of the FBI." FBI Homepage. Retrieved September 2003 (http://www.fbi.gov/libref/historic/history/historymain.htm).

Lee, Christopher. "Uncertainty at Homeland Security." *Washington Post*, March 1, 2003.

"National Strategy for Homeland Security." The White House Homepage. July 2002. Retrieved July 2003 (http://www.whitehouse.gov/homeland/book).

Palattella, Ed, Scott Westcott, and Albert J. Neri. "Rising Son." *Erie Times-News*, July 2000. Retrieved September 2003 (http://www.goerie.com/risingson).

Shenon, Philip. "Domestic Security, the Line Starts Here." *New York Times*, April 6, 2003.

Williamson, Elizabeth. "First Stop Against Terrorism, Training Center Draws Crowd." *Washington Post*, July 20, 2003.

INDEX

ABOUT THE AUTHOR

Fletcher Haulley graduated from New York University where he studied history. He is also the editor of The Rosen Publishing Group's *Critical Perspectives on 9/11*.

PHOTO CREDITS

Front cover (top) photo courtesy of the Washington, D. C., Convention and Tourism Corporation; front cover (Chertoff portrait) U.S. Department of Homeland Security; front cover (all other portraits) United States Department of Defense; front and back cover (bottom), p. 1 (top and bottom), p. 4 (background full bleed image), margin photo throughout, p. 38 © Photodisc Volumes/Business and Occupations; back cover (top), p. 4 (circle) © Photodisc Blue; pp. 4–5 © Digital Vision/Industry and Technology; p. 8 © Mark Wilson/Getty Images; p. 11 U.S. Coast Guard digital photo by PA3 Dave Hardesty; p. 13 © Still Picture Branch, National Archives and Records Administration; p. 15 © National Archives and Records Administration; p. 16 © David McNew/Getty Images; p. 19 (top) © AP/Wide World Photos/Sayyid Azim; p. 19 (bottom) © AP/Wide World Photos/Rick Bowmer; pp. 23, 55 © Reuters NewMedia Inc./Corbis; p. 25 U.S. Coast Guard digital photo by PA3 Mike Hvozda; p. 28 © LOC/Acme Newspapers, Inc., Telephoto/New York World-Telegram & Sun Collection; p. 31 © AP/Wide World Photos/Stringer; p. 32 © Brooks Kraft/Corbis; p. 37 © U.S. Department of Homeland Security; p. 42 © AP/Wide World Photos/ Nick Ut; pp. 43, 51 © Getty Images; p. 45 © AP/Wide World Photos/ Jacqueline Roggenbrodt; p. 46 © AP/Wide World Photos/Gerald Herbert; p. 49 Department of Energy Photo.

Designer: Evelyn Horovicz